WELCOME TO THE U.S.A.
LOUISIANA

Written by Ann Heinrichs   Illustrated by Matt Kania
Content Adviser: Greg Lambousy, Director of Collections,
Louisiana State Museum, New Orleans, Louisiana

The Child's World

Published in the United States of America by The Child's World®
PO Box 326 • Chanhassen, MN 55317-0326
800-599-READ • www.childsworld.com

Photo Credits

Cover: Medioimages; frontispiece: Steve Allen/Brand X Pictures.

Interior: Corbis: 10 (Richard A. Cooke), 34 (William Manning); Downtown on the Bayou: 18; Getty Images: 22 (Stone/Cosmo Condina), 30 (Time Life Pictures/ Ovoworks/Brian Miller), 31 (Hulton|Archive); Philip Gould/Corbis: 13, 21, 26; Louisiana Office of Tourism: 6, 17, 23, 25; Louisiana State Oil & Gas Museum: 29; G. Conrad Speyrer/Tony Chachere's Creole Foods: 33; US Fish and Wildlife Service: 9; LaShunda Walker/Vermilionville: 14.

Acknowledgments

The Child's World®: Mary Berendes, Publishing Director

Editorial Directions, Inc.: E. Russell Primm, Editorial Director; Katie Marsico, Associate Editor; Judith Shiffer, Assistant Editor; Matt Messbarger, Editorial Assistant; Susan Hindman, Copy Editor; Melissa McDaniel, Proofreader; Kevin Cunningham, Peter Garnham, Matt Messbarger, Olivia Nellums, Chris Simms, Molly Symmonds, Katherine Trickle, Carl Stephen Wender, Fact Checkers; Tim Griffin/IndexServ, Indexer; Cian Loughlin O'Day, Photo Researcher and Editor

The Design Lab: Kathleen Petelinsek, Design and art production

Library of Congress Cataloging-in-Publication Data
Heinrichs, Ann.
   Louisiana / by Ann Heinrichs.
      p. cm. — (Welcome to the U.S.A.)
   Includes index.
   ISBN 1-59296-376-5 (library bound : alk. paper) 1. Louisiana—Juvenile literature.
   I. Title. II. Series.
   F369.3.H45 2006
   976.3—dc22   2004026166

Ann Heinrichs is the author of more than 100 books for children and young adults. She has also enjoyed successful careers as a children's book editor and an advertising copywriter. Ann grew up in Fort Smith, Arkansas, and lives in Chicago, Illinois.

About the Author
Ann Heinrichs

Matt Kania loves maps and, as a kid, dreamed of making them. In school he studied geography and cartography, and today he makes maps for a living. Matt's favorite thing about drawing maps is learning about the places they represent. Many of the maps he has created can be found in books, magazines, videos, Web sites, and public places.

About the
Map Illustrator
Matt Kania

On the cover: **Oak Alley Plantation is located between New Orleans and Baton Rouge.**
On page one: **Bourbon Street is a popular tourist attraction.**

OUR LOUISIANA TRIP

Louisiana's Nickname: The Pelican State

Want to see things you've never seen before?

Want to hear, smell, and taste new things?

Just take a trip around Louisiana!

You'll see alligators and learn about swamp monsters.

You'll eat crawfish and **gumbo.** You'll dress up like a

pirate. Or maybe you'd rather dress like a carnival queen.

You'll meet great folks such as Louis Armstrong. You might

even learn to dance the two-step.

Are you ready to hit the road? Then buckle up—we're

on our way!

WELCOME TO LOUISIANA

As you travel through Louisiana, watch for all the interesting facts along the way.

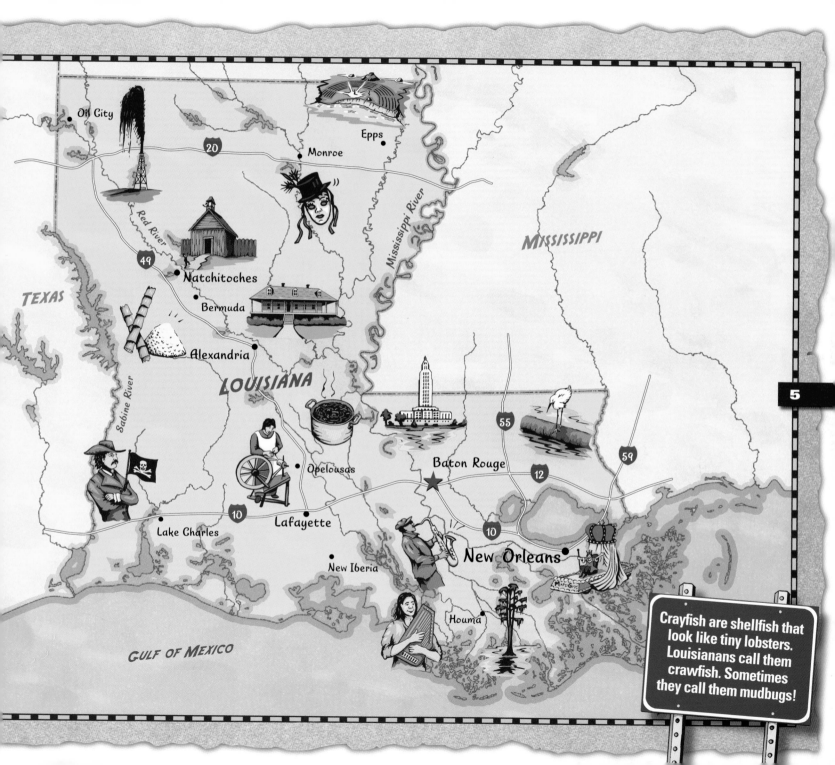

Oil City

20

Epps

Monroe

MISSISSIPPI

Red River

49

TEXAS

Natchitoches

Bermuda

Alexandria

LOUISIANA

Sabine River

Opelousas

10

Lake Charles

Lafayette

Baton Rouge

55

12

59

10

New Orleans

New Iberia

Houma

GULF OF MEXICO

Mississippi River

Crayfish are shellfish that look like tiny lobsters. Louisianans call them crawfish. Sometimes they call them mudbugs!

6

Watch out! You're touring Bayou Segnette. Is the Roux-Ga-Roux hiding behind that cypress tree?

The Mississippi River is the longest river in the United States. It begins in Minnesota.

Do you like scary stories? Then you'll love tales about the Roux-Ga-Roux. This swamp monster may sneak up and snatch you!

You can hear all about the Roux-Ga-Roux. Just take a swamp tour in Bayou Segnette.

What is a bayou? It's a slow-moving waterway. Southern Louisiana has lots of bayous. Much of this region is wet and swampy. Low, rolling hills stretch across northern Louisiana.

The Mississippi River is the state's major river. It reaches the Gulf of Mexico near New Orleans. Land near the river is called the Mississippi Delta. Soil in the Delta is very fertile. You won't find any monsters there!

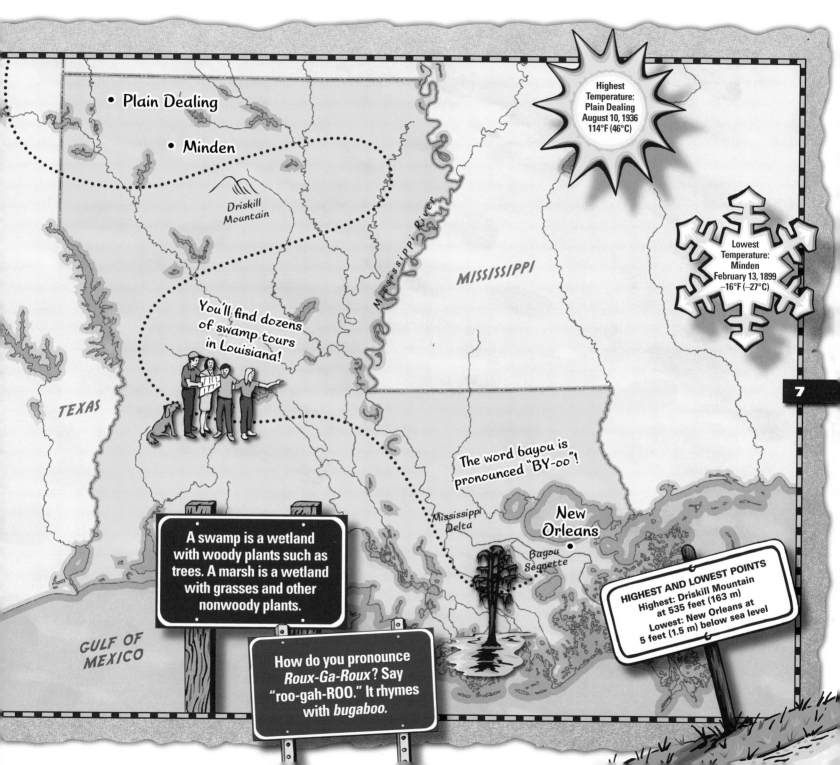

• Plain Dealing

• Minden

Driskill Mountain

TEXAS

Mississippi River

MISSISSIPPI

You'll find dozens of swamp tours in Louisiana!

The word bayou is pronounced "BY-oo"!

Mississippi Delta

New Orleans

Bayou Segnette

Highest Temperature: Plain Dealing August 10, 1936 114°F (46°C)

Lowest Temperature: Minden February 13, 1899 −16°F (−27°C)

A swamp is a wetland with woody plants such as trees. A marsh is a wetland with grasses and other nonwoody plants.

GULF OF MEXICO

How do you pronounce *Roux-Ga-Roux*? Say "roo-gah-ROO." It rhymes with *bugaboo*.

HIGHEST AND LOWEST POINTS
Highest: Driskill Mountain at 535 feet (163 m)
Lowest: New Orleans at 5 feet (1.5 m) below sea level

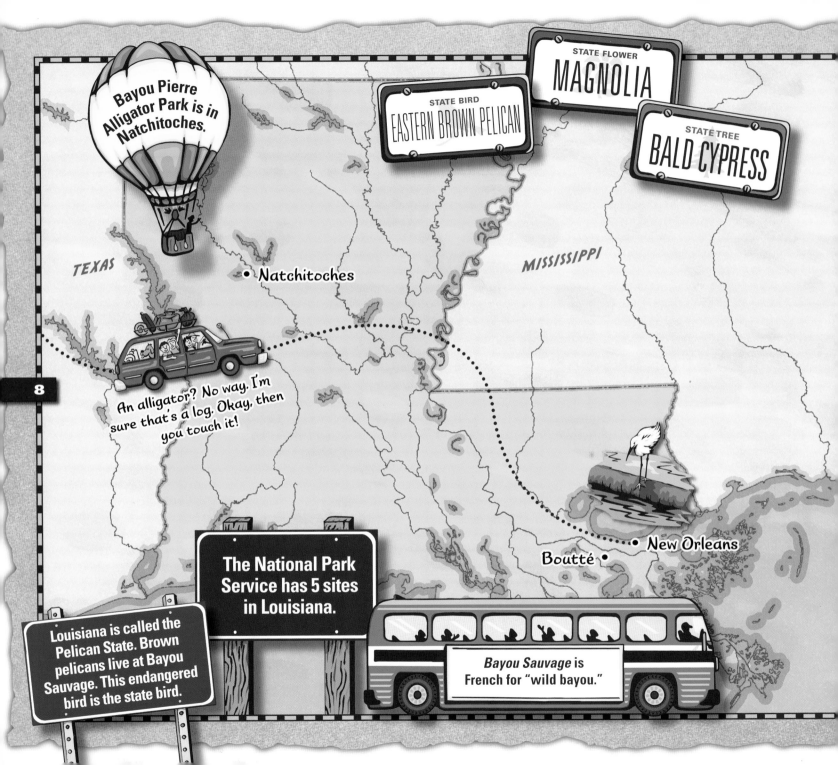

Bayou Pierre Alligator Park is in Natchitoches.

STATE BIRD
EASTERN BROWN PELICAN

STATE FLOWER
MAGNOLIA

STATE TREE
BALD CYPRESS

TEXAS

MISSISSIPPI

• Natchitoches

An alligator? No way. I'm sure that's a log. Okay, then you touch it!

• New Orleans

Boutté •

The National Park Service has 5 sites in Louisiana.

Louisiana is called the Pelican State. Brown pelicans live at Bayou Sauvage. This endangered bird is the state bird.

Bayou Sauvage is French for "wild bayou."

Bayou Sauvage National Wildlife Refuge

This gator makes its home in Bayou Sauvage.

You're gliding along in a boat. Tall cypress trees tower overhead. Long strands of Spanish moss are hanging down. Something long and lumpy is on the bank. Is it a log? No, it's an alligator!

You're in Bayou Sauvage near New Orleans. It's a national wildlife refuge. Louisiana's bayous and swamps are full of wildlife. Alligators, turtles, and snakes lurk in the shadows. Herons and egrets catch fish along the bank. These long-legged birds are built for wading. Minks and raccoons scurry in the leaves. They have to watch out for wildcats!

About half the state is forestland. Rabbits and deer find shelter in these forests. Even wild hogs live there.

Boutté holds an alligator festival every year. You can eat alligator meat pies, alligator burgers, and fried alligator!

The Mounds at Poverty Point

American Indians built the mounds at Poverty Point.

Imagine carrying a heavy basket of dirt. Now imagine carrying millions of those baskets! That's what people did at Poverty Point near Epps. They used the earth to build giant mounds.

One mound is shaped like a bird. Others are long, narrow piles. They stand in a curve, like the letter C.

People lived here more than 3,000 years ago. They hunted and fished for food. They also gathered nuts and seeds.

You can walk among the Poverty Point mounds. You can also see things that people made there. There are beads, pots, and spear points. There are also many stone birds. Owls were favorites, but no one knows why. Have any ideas?

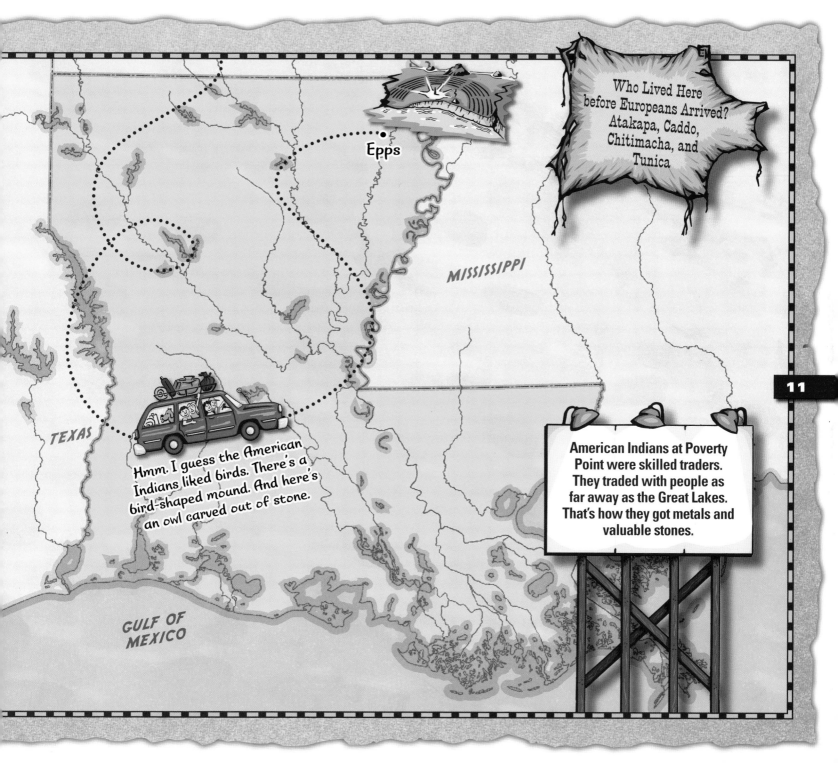

Epps

Who Lived Here before Europeans Arrived? Atakapa, Caddo, Chitimacha, and Tunica

MISSISSIPPI

TEXAS

Hmm. I guess the American Indians liked birds. There's a bird-shaped mound. And here's an owl carved out of stone.

American Indians at Poverty Point were skilled traders. They traded with people as far away as the Great Lakes. That's how they got metals and valuable stones.

GULF OF MEXICO

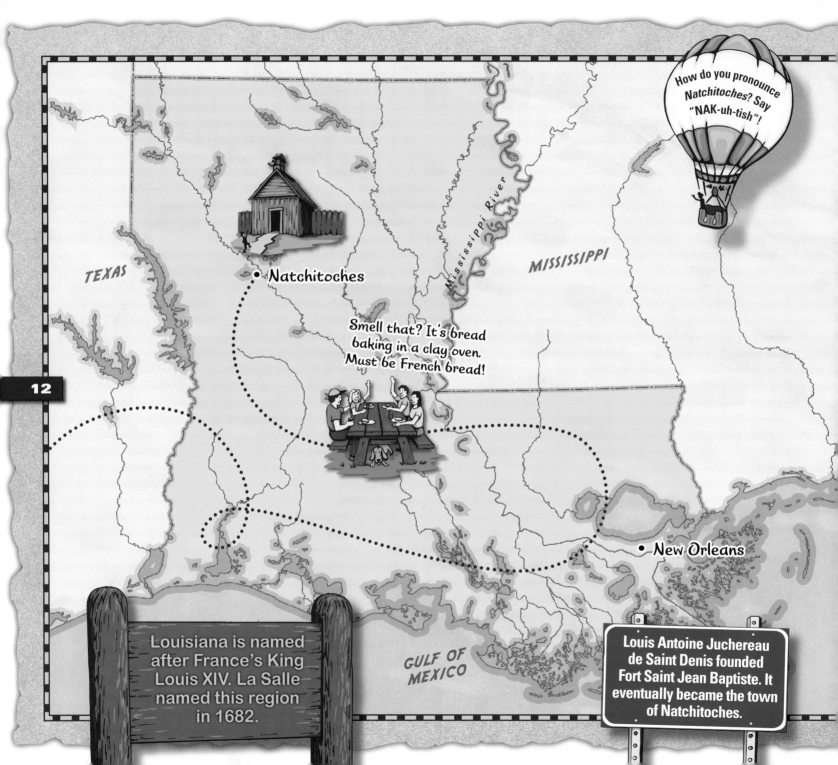

Take a trip back in time at Fort Saint Jean Baptiste! Workers there wear 1700s clothing.

13

Log cabins are everywhere at Fort Saint Jean Baptiste. Living-history weekends there are great fun. Everyone's dressed like a French person in the 1700s. Why is that?

French people from Canada explored Louisiana. One was René-Robert Cavelier, Sieur de la Salle. He came down the Mississippi River in 1682. Soon traders and fur trappers arrived. Fort Saint Jean Baptiste was Louisiana's earliest settlement. A French trader settled it in 1714.

Louisiana passed to Spain and then back to France. The United States bought Louisiana in 1803. This was called the Louisiana Purchase. Steamboats started chugging down the Mississippi River.

La Salle claimed the whole Mississippi River valley for France. That included more than 12 present-day states!

14

A woman spins cotton at Vermilionville. Visitors learn what life was like for Louisiana's Acadians.

A blacksmith hammers out an iron tool. A woman spins cotton at her spinning wheel. A woodworker carves a cypress wood cabinet.

These are daily activities at Vermilionville. This park is like an old Acadian village. Acadians were early settlers in Louisiana.

The first Acadians were French people living in Canada. Their **colony** was called Acadia. British soldiers drove them out in the mid-1700s. Most Acadians settled in southern Louisiana.

In time, the word *Acadian* changed into *Cajun*. Many Cajuns settled in the bayous. They fished, hunted, and farmed. Cajuns developed special food and music. Their language is a form of French. Cajun **culture** is still a big part of life in Louisiana.

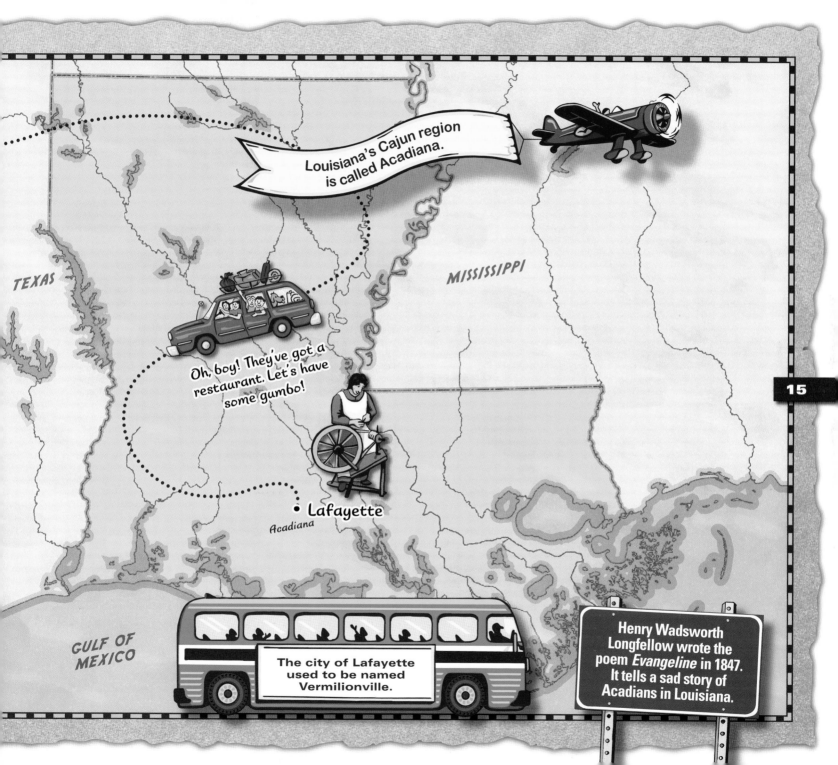

Louisiana's Cajun region is called Acadiana.

Oh, boy! They've got a restaurant. Let's have some gumbo!

TEXAS

MISSISSIPPI

Lafayette

Acadiana

GULF OF MEXICO

The city of Lafayette used to be named Vermilionville.

Henry Wadsworth Longfellow wrote the poem *Evangeline* in 1847. It tells a sad story of Acadians in Louisiana.

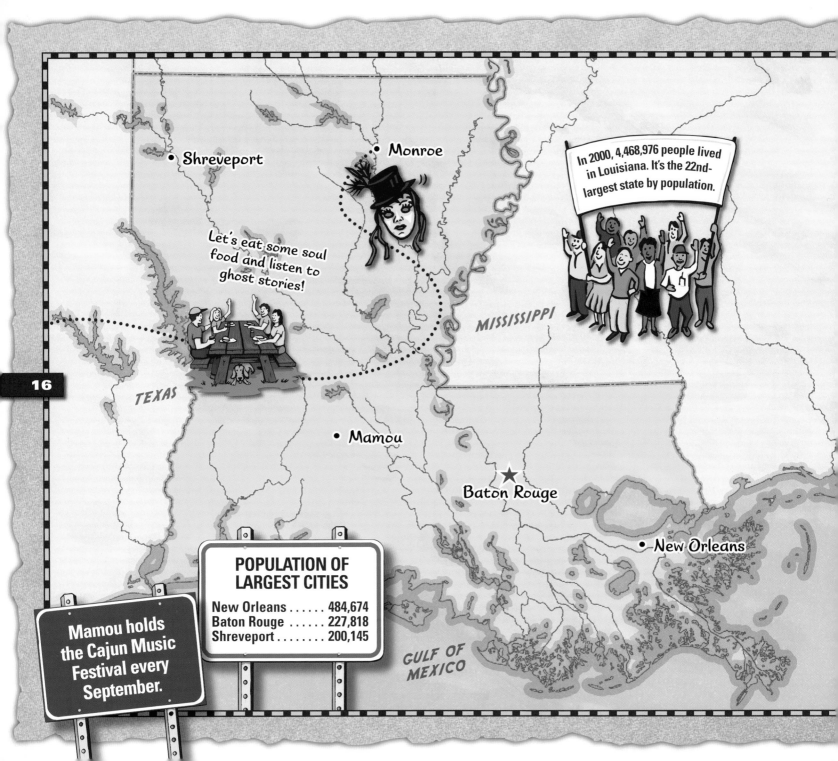

O ver there, you might hear ghost stories. Over here, enjoy some **jambalaya.** Here's a fiddler, and there's a mask maker.

You're at the Louisiana Folklife Festival. It offers the best of Louisiana's many **traditions.**

Lots of different **ethnic** groups live in Louisiana. Cajuns and Creoles live in southern Louisiana. Creoles have a mix of backgrounds. Their **ancestors** were African, French, or Spanish settlers.

About one out of three Louisianans is African American. Other people have roots in Hispanic or Asian lands. Each group has special music, foods, crafts, and stories. Come to the festival and enjoy them all!

Want to dance? There's plenty of music to enjoy at the Folklife Festival!

17

Ready, set, go! Louisiana boaters compete in a pirogue race.

18

People are paddling around in pirogues. Those are Cajun canoes. They're made of hollowed-out logs. The boaters have bags over their heads. People onshore are yelling which way to go!

This race is called the Human Race. It's part of the Downtown on the Bayou Festival. That's one of Louisiana's many Cajun festivals.

A Cajun wedding takes place there, too. Then Cajun musicians play the fiddle, accordion, and triangle. Go ahead and try the Cajun two-step!

There's plenty of Cajun food on hand. Have some red beans and rice. Or maybe you'd like a shrimp po-boy. That's a shrimp sandwich on French bread!

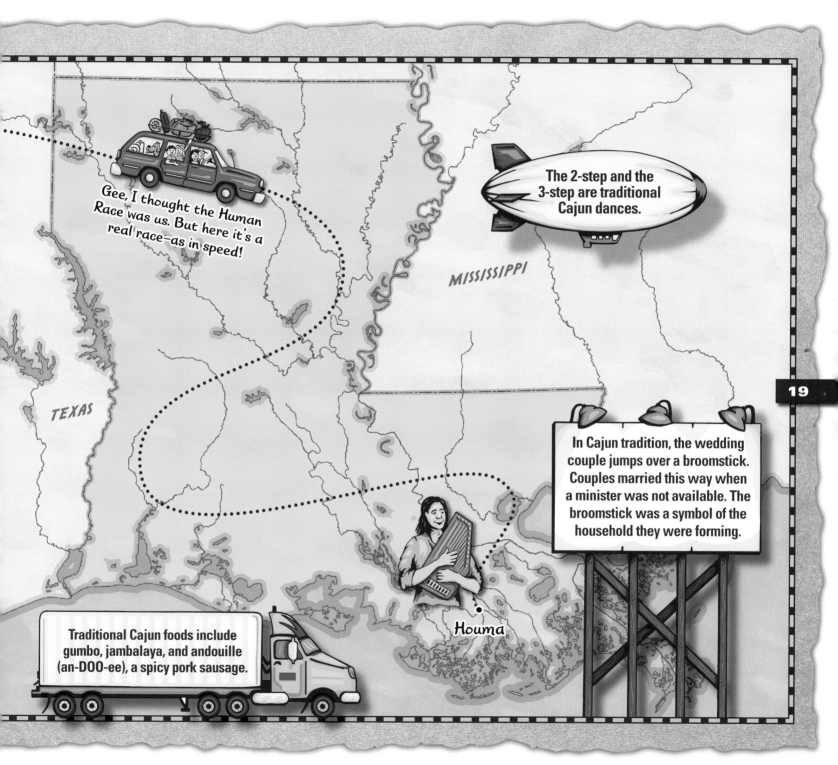

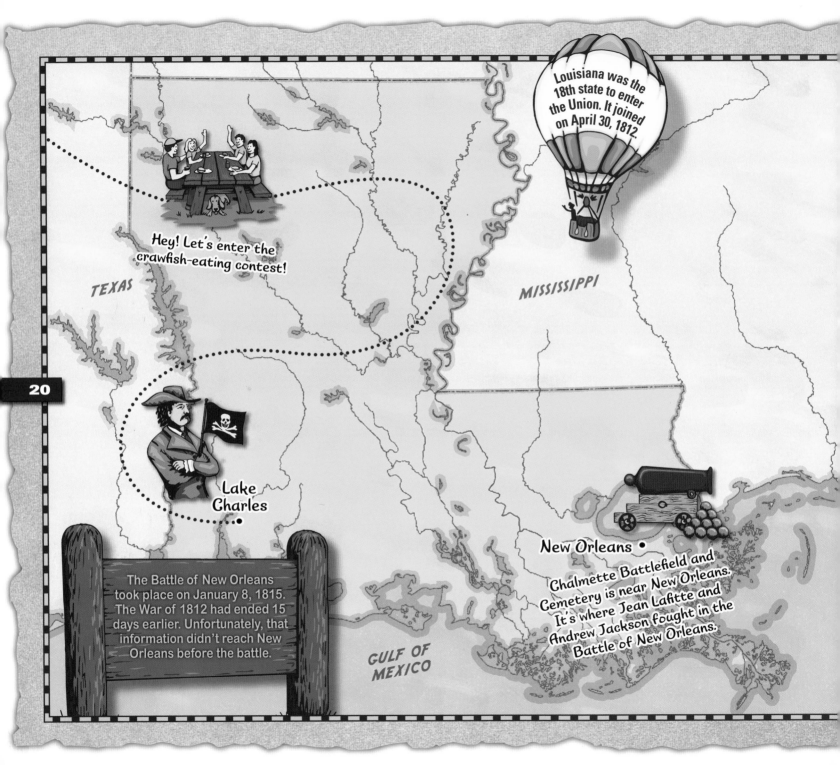

Contraband Days in Lake Charles

Put on your black eye patch. Paint on some tattoos. Maybe you'll win the pirate costume contest! You're at Lake Charles's Contraband Days festival. It celebrates the days of Jean Lafitte.

Lafitte was a famous pirate. He and his crew attacked ships off Louisiana's coast. They stole the valuable goods onboard. They also sold illegal goods, or contraband.

Lafitte had a good side, too. He helped out in the War of 1812. The United States fought Great Britain in this war.

British soldiers attacked U.S. troops near New Orleans. Lafitte helped General Andrew Jackson win the battle. Then Lafitte became a hero!

Are you at a circus? No! Contraband Days features many colorful and creative costumes.

21

Do you like jazz? Then New Orleans is the place for you!

22

Sniff the air in New Orleans. You'll probably smell something delicious! French pastry shops are everywhere. Lots of restaurants serve Cajun or Creole foods. These foods are famous for being really spicy.

New Orleans is a great place to explore. Some sections look like an old European city. The French Quarter was originally built in the 1700s. Its narrow buildings have fancy iron **balconies.**

You're sure to hear music in the air, too. People say jazz was born in New Orleans. Many famous jazz musicians once played there. One was trumpet player Louis Armstrong. He sure could blow that horn!

The 1st public subscription library in Louisiana opened in New Orleans in 1805.

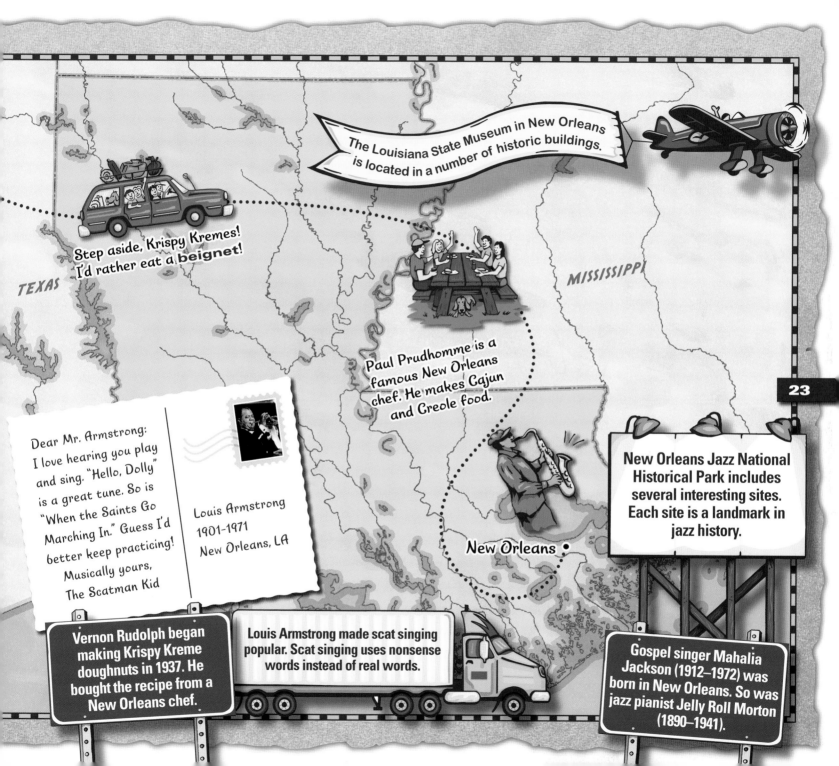

The Louisiana State Museum in New Orleans is located in a number of historic buildings.

Step aside, Krispy Kremes! I'd rather eat a **beignet**!

TEXAS

MISSISSIPPI

Paul Prudhomme is a famous New Orleans chef. He makes Cajun and Creole food.

23

Dear Mr. Armstrong:
I love hearing you play and sing. "Hello, Dolly" is a great tune. So is "When the Saints Go Marching In." Guess I'd better keep practicing!
Musically yours,
The Scatman Kid

Louis Armstrong
1901–1971
New Orleans, LA

New Orleans Jazz National Historical Park includes several interesting sites. Each site is a landmark in jazz history.

New Orleans

Vernon Rudolph began making Krispy Kreme doughnuts in 1937. He bought the recipe from a New Orleans chef.

Louis Armstrong made scat singing popular. Scat singing uses nonsense words instead of real words.

Gospel singer Mahalia Jackson (1912–1972) was born in New Orleans. So was jazz pianist Jelly Roll Morton (1890–1941).

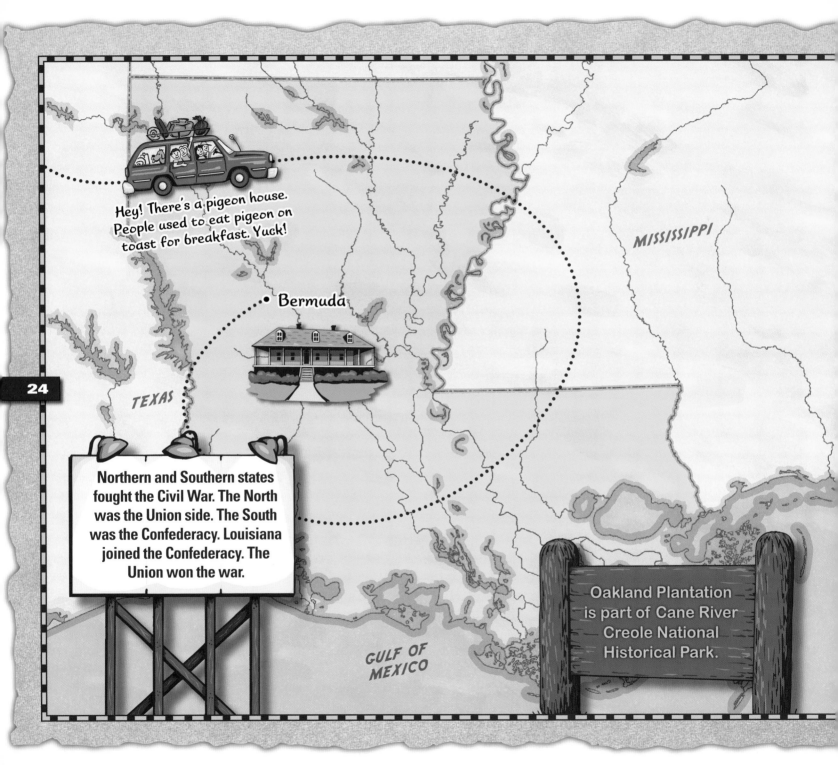

Hey! There's a pigeon house. People used to eat pigeon on toast for breakfast. Yuck!

MISSISSIPPI

• Bermuda

TEXAS

Northern and Southern states fought the Civil War. The North was the Union side. The South was the Confederacy. Louisiana joined the Confederacy. The Union won the war.

GULF OF MEXICO

Oakland Plantation is part of Cane River Creole National Historical Park.

How would you like living on a **plantation**? To find out, just visit Oakland Plantation.

You'll see kids' bedrooms in the main house. Kids slept in **canopy beds** or **trundle beds.** Many other buildings are located in the back. One is a house for pigeons!

Louisiana had several plantations in the 1800s. African slaves did much of the labor. Oakland Plantation raised cotton for cloth. Many other plantations raised sugarcane.

Slaves were freed after the Civil War (1861–1865). After that, tenant farmers worked the land. These farmers could sell the crops they raised. They then paid rent to the plantation owners.

What was life like in Louisiana during the 1800s? Tour scenic Oakland Plantation and learn for yourself!

A Louisiana farmer harvests sugarcane.

Kent Plantation is in Alexandria. It was a working sugarcane plantation in the 1800s.

Sugar Day at Kent Plantation

Brown juice is boiling in big kettles. The juice is cane syrup. The kettles are as big as bathtubs!

It's Sugar Day at Kent Plantation. This festival celebrates old-time sugar-making days. Sugar comes from the sugarcane plant. That's still Louisiana's top crop.

How did people turn sugarcane into sugar? First, they pressed juice out of sugarcane stalks. Then they boiled the juice. It became thick, sweet cane syrup. Next, the syrup was dried. This left brown chunks of raw sugar.

A few more steps produced white sugar grains. Sugar is made much the same way today. Do you sprinkle sugar on your cereal? You'll have a lot to think about now!

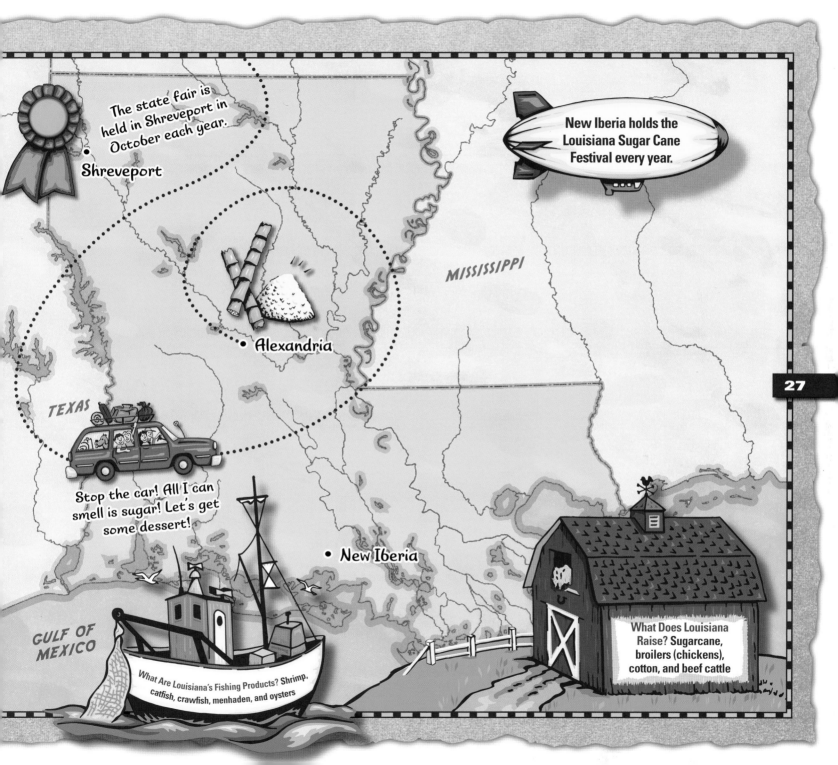

The state fair is held in Shreveport in October each year.

Shreveport

New Iberia holds the Louisiana Sugar Cane Festival every year.

MISSISSIPPI

Alexandria

TEXAS

Stop the car! All I can smell is sugar! Let's get some dessert!

New Iberia

GULF OF MEXICO

What Are Louisiana's Fishing Products? Shrimp, catfish, crawfish, menhaden, and oysters

What Does Louisiana Raise? Sugarcane, broilers (chickens), cotton, and beef cattle

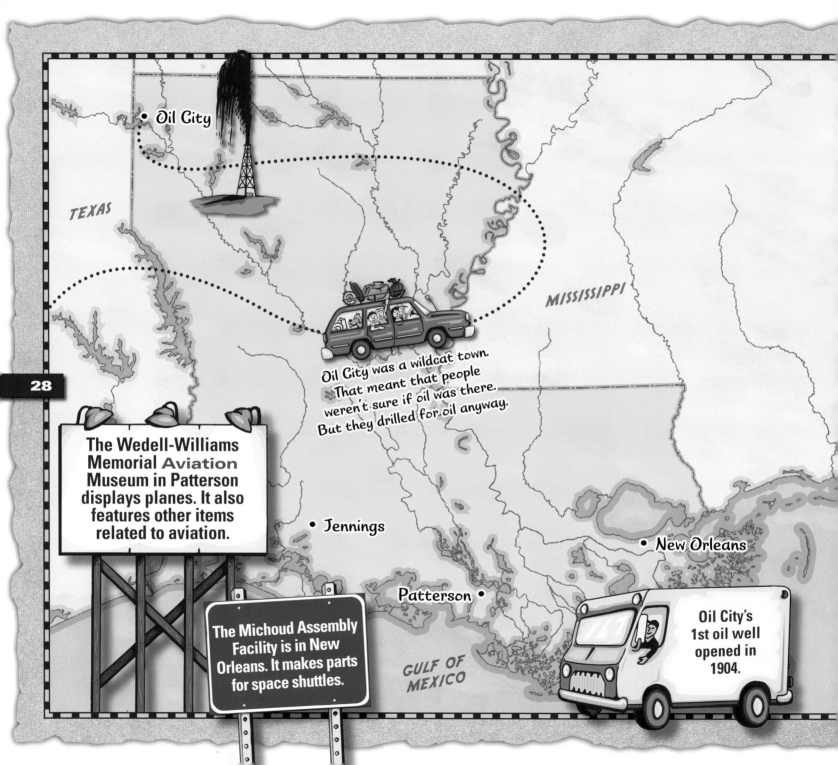

• Oil City

TEXAS

MISSISSIPPI

Oil City was a wildcat town. That meant that people weren't sure if oil was there. But they drilled for oil anyway.

The Wedell-Williams Memorial Aviation Museum in Patterson displays planes. It also features other items related to aviation.

• Jennings

• New Orleans

The Michoud Assembly Facility is in New Orleans. It makes parts for space shuttles.

Patterson •

GULF OF MEXICO

Oil City's 1st oil well opened in 1904.

Oil City's Oil and Gas Museum

Oil City was once a pretty wild place. Oil was discovered there in the early 1900s. Soon thousands of people went there to work. Some lived in shacks. They slept on metal beds. Others lived in tents. People hung out at the saloon. Sometimes troublemakers got into fights.

Want to learn more about this time period? Just visit Oil City's Oil and Gas Museum!

Oil became a big **industry** in Louisiana. Another big industry began in the 1960s—space! Louisiana began making Saturn rockets. One rocket boosted *Apollo 11* into space in 1969. Its astronauts landed on the Moon!

Visitors explore the Oil and Gas Museum. The Petroleum Gallery is filled with several interesting exhibits.

Louisiana's 1st oil well was drilled in 1901 near Jennings.

30

Baton Rouge's skyscraper capitol shines against the night sky.

Welcome to Baton Rouge, the capital of Louisiana!

Stand in front of Louisiana's state capitol. You'll notice something right away. There's no big, curved dome on top. This capitol is a skyscraper. It's the tallest state capitol in the country!

Inside the capitol are state government offices. Louisiana's government is divided into three branches. One branch makes the state's laws. Another branch carries out those laws. It's headed by the governor. The third branch is made up of judges. They decide whether someone has broken a law.

Huey Long was a famous Louisiana governor. It was his idea to build the skyscraper capitol.

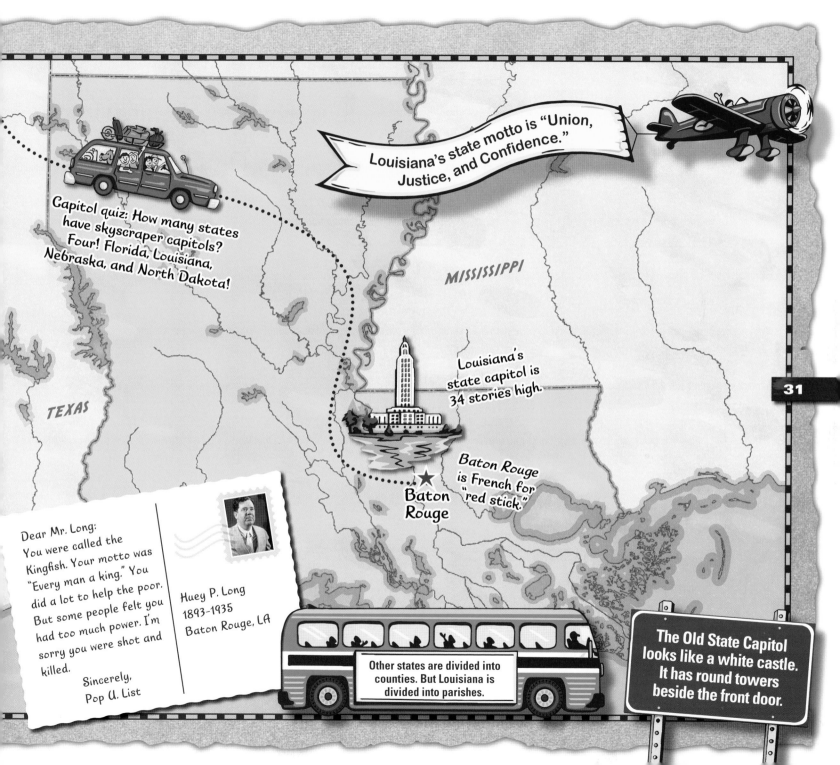

Louisiana's state motto is "Union, Justice, and Confidence."

Capitol quiz: How many states have skyscraper capitols? Four! Florida, Louisiana, Nebraska, and North Dakota!

MISSISSIPPI

Louisiana's state capitol is 34 stories high.

TEXAS

Baton Rouge is French for "red stick."

★ Baton Rouge

Dear Mr. Long:
You were called the Kingfish. Your motto was "Every man a king." You did a lot to help the poor. But some people felt you had too much power. I'm sorry you were shot and killed.

Sincerely,
Pop U. List

Huey P. Long
1893–1935
Baton Rouge, LA

Other states are divided into counties. But Louisiana is divided into parishes.

The Old State Capitol looks like a white castle. It has round towers beside the front door.

Making Spicy Food in Opelousas

Smell the spices. Watch machines whir and blend. Hoppers are dropping tons of beans and rice. They're mixing up Creole and Cajun foods. Once they're ready, meals are packaged up and shipped off. This is Tony Chachere's food plant!

Foods are important factory products in Louisiana. Food factories start out with a farm product. They may clean, boil, chop, or package it. Then it can be sold in stores. Coffee, sugar, and soft drinks are a few examples. So are baked goods and hot sauce.

Louisiana factories also make oil and coal products. Some make medicine, paint, soap, or cardboard. Louisiana builds huge ships, too.

Hope you're in the mood for something spicy! Tony Chachere's plant makes tasty Creole seasoning.

Tony Chachere (1905-1995) was nicknamed the Ole Master. He was the 1st person admitted to the Louisiana Chefs Hall of Fame.

Mardi Gras World in New Orleans

These colorful decorations are housed at Mardi Gras World.

Mardi Gras is French for "Fat Tuesday." That's the day before Lent begins. Lent is a traditional Christian season before Easter. It's a time for cutting down on food.

Everywhere you look, there's something big and shiny. Here's a sea monster and a fierce alligator. There's a giant **jester** with bells on his hat.

You're at Mardi Gras World in New Orleans. It's sort of like a factory. It makes decorations for the city's biggest event.

Mardi Gras is a huge carnival. People wear costumes and dance in the streets. Parades with giant floats go by. Each float may have a fancy king or queen. They throw bead necklaces to the crowds. The streets get pretty crowded during Mardi Gras. Everyone is bumping into each other! That's why it's fun to visit Mardi Gras World. You can enjoy the awesome sights in peace!

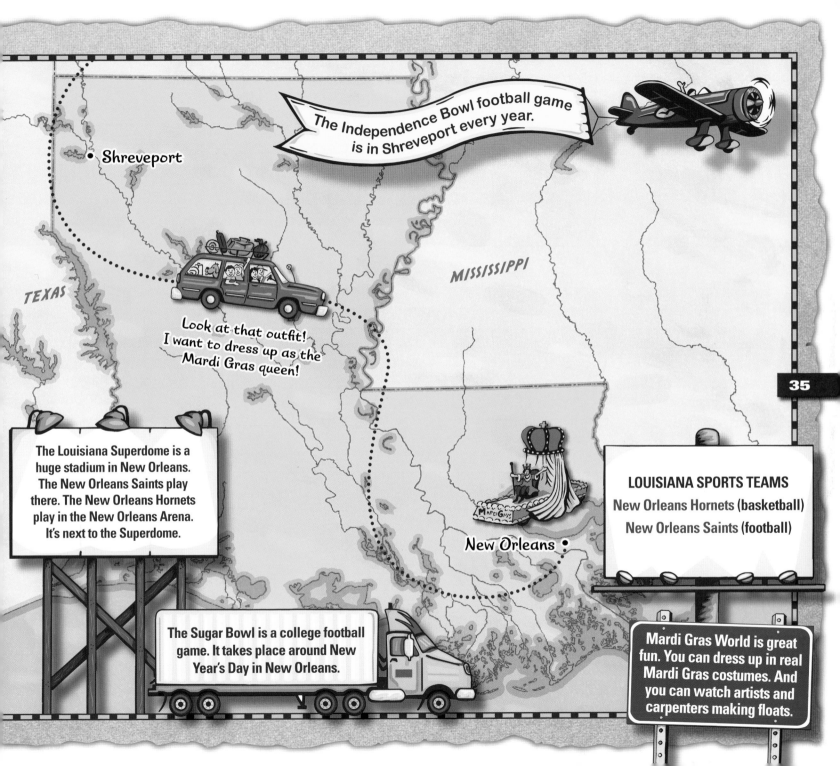

The Independence Bowl football game is in Shreveport every year.

Shreveport

TEXAS

MISSISSIPPI

Look at that outfit! I want to dress up as the Mardi Gras queen!

The Louisiana Superdome is a huge stadium in New Orleans. The New Orleans Saints play there. The New Orleans Hornets play in the New Orleans Arena. It's next to the Superdome.

New Orleans

LOUISIANA SPORTS TEAMS
New Orleans Hornets (basketball)
New Orleans Saints (football)

The Sugar Bowl is a college football game. It takes place around New Year's Day in New Orleans.

Mardi Gras World is great fun. You can dress up in real Mardi Gras costumes. And you can watch artists and carpenters making floats.

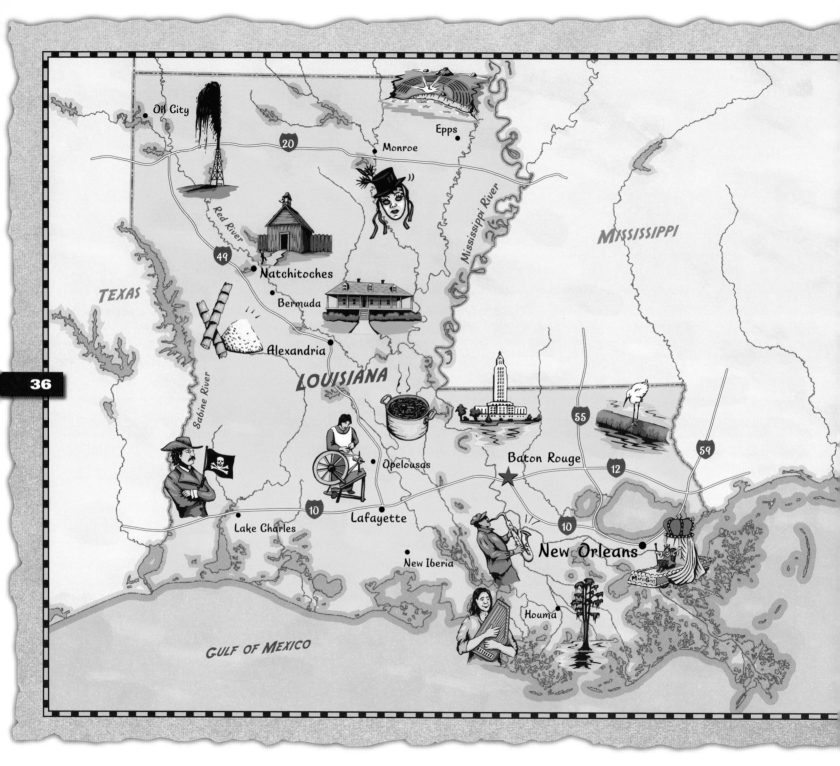

OUR TRIP

We visited many amazing places on our trip! We also met a lot of interesting people along the way. Look at the map on the left. Use your finger to trace all the places we have been.

Where does the Mississippi River begin? See page 6 for the answer.

How did the Indians at Poverty Point get metal and valuable stones? Page 11 has the answer.

Who is Louisiana named after? See page 12 for the answer.

How many people lived in Louisiana in 2000? Look on page 16 for the answer.

What are 3 traditional Cajun foods? Page 19 has the answer.

How old was Louis Armstrong when he died? Turn to page 23 for the answer.

What are broilers? Look on page 27 and find out!

What is Louisiana's state motto? Turn to page 31 for the answer.

That was a great trip! We have traveled all over Louisiana!

There are a few places that we didn't have time for, though. Next time, we plan to visit the Bayou Pierre Alligator Park in Nachitoches. Visitors can watch the alligators being fed. They can also see alligator training in the swamp.

More Places to Visit in Louisiana

WORDS TO KNOW

ancestors (AN-sess-turz) grandparents, great-grandparents, and earlier relatives

aviation (ay-vee-AY-shuhn) building and flying airplanes

balconies (BAL-kuh-neez) platforms that stick out from a building and have railings

beignet (behn-YAY) a square doughnut with no hole

canopy beds (KAN-uh-pee BEDZ) beds with a cloth covering hanging above them

colony (KOL-uh-nee) a new land with ties to a parent country

culture (KUHL-chur) a group's customs, beliefs, and way of life

ethnic (ETH-nik) having to do with a person's race or nationality

gumbo (GUHM-boh) thick soup made with okra, a gooey vegetable

industry (IN-duh-stree) a type of business

jambalaya (jum-buh-LYE-uh) spicy stew with rice, meat, and vegetables

jester (JES-tur) a person in a funny suit whose job is to entertain kings and queens

plantation (plan-TAY-shuhn) a large farm that raises mainly 1 crop

traditions (truh-DISH-uhnz) customs handed down from generation to generation

trundle beds (TRUHN-duhl BEDZ) low beds that slide under regular beds

Louisiana covers 43,562 square miles (112,825 sq km). It's the 33rd-largest state in size.

STATE SYMBOLS

State amphibian: Green tree frog

State bird: Brown pelican

State colors: Blue, white, and gold

State crustacean: Crawfish

State dog: Catahoula leopard dog

State drink: Milk

State flower: Magnolia

State fossil: Petrified palmwood

State freshwater fish: White perch

State gemstone: Agate

State insect: Honeybee

State mammal: Black bear

State musical instrument: Diatonic accordion (Cajun accordion)

State reptile: Alligator

State tree: Bald cypress

State wildflower: Louisiana iris

State flag

State seal

STATE SONG

"Give Me Louisiana"

Words and music by Doralice Fontane

Give me Louisiana,
The state where I was born
The state of snowy cotton,
The best I've ever known;
A state of sweet magnolias,
And creole melodies
Oh give me Louisiana,
The state where I was born
Oh what sweet old memories
The mossy old oaks bring
It brings us the story of our
   Evangeline
A state of old tradition,
Of old plantation days
Makes good old Louisiana
The sweetest of all states.

Give me Louisiana,
A state prepared to share
That good old southern custom,
Hospitality so rare;
A state of fruit and flowers,
Of sunshine and spring showers
Oh give me Louisiana,
The state where I was born.

Its woodlands, its marshes
Where humble trappers live
Its rivers, its valleys,
A place to always give
A state where work is pleasure,
With blessings in full measure
Makes good old Louisiana
The dearest of all states.

Give me Louisiana,
Where love birds always sing
In shady lanes or pastures,
The cowbells softly ring;
The softness of the sunset
Brings peace and blissful rest
Oh give me Louisiana,
The state where I was born.
The smell of sweet clover
Which blossoms everywhere
The fresh new mown hay
Where children romp and play
A state of love and laughter,
A state for all here after
Makes good old Louisiana
The grandest of all states.

FAMOUS PEOPLE

Armstrong, Louis (1901–1971), musician and singer

Audubon, John James (1785–1851), naturalist and artist

Beene, Geoffrey (1927–), fashion designer

Capote, Truman (1924–1984), author

Carville, James (1944–), political adviser and author

Chopin, Kate (1850–1904), author

Domino, Fats (1928–), singer

Hellman, Lillian (1905–1984), playwright

Jackson, Mahalia (1911–1972), singer

Lamour, Dorothy (1914–1996), actor

Lewis, Jerry Lee (1935–), singer

Marsalis, Wynton (1961–), trumpet player

Morton, Jelly Roll (1890–1941), jazz musician

Newton, Huey P. (1942–1989), African American activist

Roberts, Cokie (1943–), journalist

Saxon, Elizabeth Lyle (1832–1915), women's rights activist

Spears, Britney (1981–), singer

Stewart, Kordell (1972–), football player

Taylor, Zachary (1784–1850), 12th U.S. president

White, Edward Douglass (1845–1921), U.S. Supreme Court justice

TO FIND OUT MORE

At the Library

Couvillon, Alice, Elizabeth Moore, and Marilyn Carter Rougelot (illustrator). *Mimi's First Mardi Gras*. Gretna, La.: Pelican Publishing Company, 1992.

Fahlenkamp-Merrell, Kindle. *Louis Armstrong*. Chanhassen, Minn.: The Child's World, 2002.

Prieto, Anita C., and Laura Knorr (illustrator). *P Is for Pelican: A Louisiana Alphabet*. Chelsea, Mich.: Sleeping Bear Press, 2003.

On the Web

Visit our home page for lots of links about Louisiana:
http://www.childsworld.com/links

Note to Parents, Teachers, and Librarians: We routinely verify our Web links to make sure they are safe, active sites—so encourage your readers to check them out!

Places to Visit or Contact

Louisiana Office of Tourism
PO Box 94291
Baton Rouge, LA 70804
225/342-8100
For more information about traveling in Louisiana

Louisiana State Museum
751 Chartres
New Orleans, LA 70116
504/568-6968
For more information about the history of Louisiana

INDEX

Bye, Pelican State.
We had a great time.
We'll come back soon!